FLOWERS FOR
FOUR WEDDINGS

Flowers for
Four Weddings

Simon Lycett

CLARKSON POTTER / PUBLISHERS NEW YORK

For my parents, John and Judith Lycett, for their love,
support and understanding, who have given me so much
and for letting me be who I am today.

Published by Clarkson N. Potter, Inc., Publishers,
201 East 50th Street, New York, New York 10022.
Member of the Crown Publishing Group.

Random House, Inc. New York, Toronto, London, Sydney, Auckland
Originally published in Great Britain by Ebury Press

CLARKSON N. POTTER, POTTER, and colophon are trademarks
of Clarkson N. Potter, Inc.

Color separations produced in Italy by Colorlito Rigogliosi, Milan
Manufactured in Italy

Edited by Margot Richardson
Design by Sue Storey, Patrick McLeavey and Partners
Photographs by Sandra Lane
Four Weddings and a Funeral film pictures by Stephen Morley, reprinted
by kind permission of PolyGram Filmed Entertainment © PolyGram
Filmed Entertainment 1995

Library of Congress Cataloging-in-Publication Data for this book is
available upon request

ISBN 0-517-70345-9

10 9 8 7 6 5 4 3 2 1

First American Edition

*PREVIOUS PAGE This charming headdress incorporating pink roses can be
made in the same way as the headdress featured on pages 62-65. It would be
suitable either for a bride, or bridesmaids.*

CONTENTS

INTRODUCTION

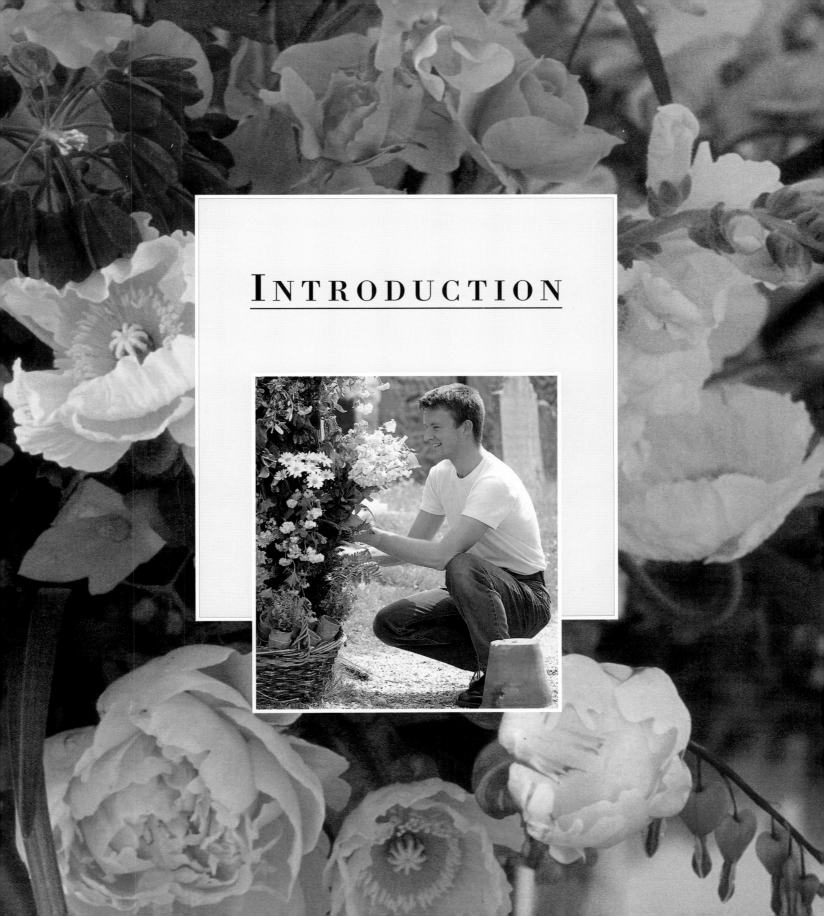

'We're making this film about four weddings . . .'

In January of 1993, I received a telephone call from Maggie Grey, the production designer on *Four Weddings and a Funeral*. She had been given my name by Duncan Kenworthy, the producer. She said that they were making a film about weddings, and that she would like to talk to me about the flowers. And so it was that I became involved in what was to become one of the most successful British films ever made.

Flowers to decorate a wedding venue need not be formal and stiff. Contemporary trends favour a more natural and relaxed look.

The first meeting was at Shepperton Studios. I met Maggie, and Anna Pinnock, the buyer and set designer. The three of us clicked immediately and I was given a script to read, in order to come back to them with my own ideas.

At the time I was very busy working on a shoot for *Brides* magazine, on location at Castle Ashby in Northamptonshire. With me was a dear friend with whom I often work, Janie Heynes. I had the script with me, and one evening over a glass of wine we sat down and read it through. Before long we were both in stitches. As soon as we came to the description of the first wedding, of Laura in her wedding dress 'looking like a meringue', I knew this was something in which I wanted to be involved.

Several meetings followed, by which time it was mid-February. Filming was due to start in early May, but meanwhile I had organized

A combination of subtle colours are used in this luxurious floral chair back.

to go away to India for six weeks. It was with some trepidation that Maggie and Anna committed the floral decoration of their film to a florist who was going to be out of the country until two weeks before filming was due to start. However, it was a wonderful feeling to be going off on holiday in the knowledge that I had six weeks of exciting work on my return. It was also great to have a good rest before the filming started. From my experience of working on commercials and other smaller films I was aware that it would be hard work. Even so, I had not realized quite *how* hard it would be.

Every day, I would start from the New Covent Garden flower market in Vauxhall, South London. Terry, my driver, would meet me there with his enormous truck at 4 or 5 am. We would load up with flowers and set off in convoy for the day's location. Although all the locations were near London, they were nevertheless a solid two-hour drive away. There we would be met by the prop men – Charlie, Barry and Russell – who are worth their weight in gold. With their help, everything was unloaded, sorted out and put in water. Then the decorating would begin. Usually I had two days to prepare a location with filming starting at 8 am on the third day, by which time the whole church or reception venue had to be finished and ready for the crew and cast to move in. It was quite a nerve-racking responsibility when you realize the number of people who would be standing around idly waiting for me to finish before the camera could take over. I am proud to say that only once did I have to call for extra time, and even then only the location manager and I had to work late.

On other days, I would be at the location for the first day's filming to ensure everything was as required, to make up the bouquets and head-dresses, and buttonholes (boutonnieres) for the extras. Then, having made sure I could be reached, I would drive to the next

Bright yellow adds a cheerful and festive note to a dark church or a winter wedding.

Strong, rich colours are not often the traditional choice for weddings, but used with confidence and flair they can look extraordinarily beautiful.

location and begin propping that. However, each morning I still had to visit the filming location to check the flowers and make up that day's buttonholes and bridal flowers. I soon became excellent at orienteering, finding my way across country to the various locations with my car boot full of chicken wire and buckets, with the passenger seat covered in market receipts, empty drink cans and sandwich packets. It was one of the hottest spells of the summer of 1993 and although it was good for my tan, keeping the flowers fresh was a complete nightmare!

At the end of each day it was a very tired and sore-handed Simon who drove back home, bleary eyed, to spend an hour or more accounting for that day's petty cash expenditure and making lists of flowers and requirements for the forthcoming shots.

I had to be aware of what would be required for the Scottish wedding in three weeks' time, to order the roses or amaryllis in time to get them open, and then to re-order the same for the reception which might be filmed two weeks after the church ceremony. Continuity could have been a nightmare, but I made very careful decisions when ordering flowers to ensure that availability could be guaranteed. This was a little sad because it prevented using some of the most beautiful English seasonal flowers and foliage, but I was fearful that some of them wouldn't be around long enough to use in one wedding filmed over a period of two months.

Most days began at 3.30 or 4 am and I didn't get to bed before 11.30 pm. After a while this took its toll and I pleaded with the production office to be given an occasional overnight stay in a hotel near the location. However, finding a hotel which would accept a filthy looking and unshaven florist in the middle of Hampshire at 10 pm was no easy task. (And why are British hotels never able to offer anything more than a sandwich after about 9 pm?)

This was my life for six weeks, with only two days off in the whole period. Exhausting, yes, but hugely satisfying. My memories of the filming are of sitting in the shade of a tree in one sunny, glorious location after another, writing up my accounts or wiring up a stand-in bouquet or headdress while watching the filming or chatting to the magical girls and boys from the wardrobe and make-up departments. I made many lovely new friends and had a glorious summer with them, working on one of the funniest, most enjoyable films I have ever seen.

Thank you, Richard Curtis, for your brilliant script.

Matching flowers can be made up into corsages and buttonholes (boutonnieres). These are not expensive, and add a delightful finishing touch to the wedding decorations.

BEFORE THE
WEDDING

Planning and Organization

Before starting to decorate a church or reception venue, there are many things to remember, plan and consider. First, of course, there are the flowers themselves. You will need to decide on your style and colour scheme and ascertain what flowers are available at a reasonable cost at the time of year when the wedding is taking place. To calculate the types and quantities needed, each of the projects included in this book has a list of the flowers used, presented a little like the ingredients in a recipe.

Next, there is all the necessary equipment: suggestions are listed and explained below.

Remember to work out where the water supply is, and where you will be able to store the flowers. This must be out of direct sunlight, cool but not damp, and preferably near the car. Be prepared to take quite a while putting the flowers in water; you'll be amazed at how many buckets are needed. Large quantities of flowers are usually supplied in boxes. Once they are empty, try to break them down to avoid cluttering up your work space, but remember to keep some for carrying the flowers to the church or reception.

Tools and Equipment

ABSOLUTE ESSENTIALS
Depending on the sorts of arrangements you will be undertaking, the following will act as a useful check-list:
• Good strong buckets, both deep and shallow
• Plastic rubbish (trash) bags
• Dustpan and brush
• Broom
• Dustsheets and/or polythene sheeting
• Watering can
• Aluminium step-ladder
• Chicken wire: standard 5cm (2in) mesh wire netting is available from most hardware shops, usually in 30cm (12in)-wide rolls. It is essential that 5cm (2in) mesh is used for all of the arrangements shown in this book.
• Reel wire:
Silver: used for finer work such as headdresses, buttonholes (boutonnieres) and bouquets
Steel: used for binding flowers into garlands
Galvanized: used for fastening and securing arrangements and garlands into position
• Stub wire: 18–22 gauge, in a variety of lengths
• Pliers and/or wire cutters: useful to prevent blunting flower scissors
• Water-retaining foam (brand name Oasis): the standard size is 23 x 11 x 8 cm (9 x 4$\frac{1}{4}$ x 3$\frac{1}{2}$in), but it is also available in a variety of shapes and sizes

• Flower tape (Oasis tape): green if possible
• Oasis spade: a plant tray, rectangular in shape with a handle at one end, that holds a block of foam
• Window-box (Oasis) tray: holds soaked foam blocks in an arrangement
• Extension tubes: plastic planter cones, which once filled with water and stems of flowers or foliage, allow you to position shorter stemmed flowers higher up in an arrangement than would otherwise be possible. They also allow you to put in bunches of flowers rather than single stems which can tend to become lost in a large arrangement. Come in green or white (which is harder to hide)
• Thick black polythene: for backing moss bases

LUXURY ITEMS
The following items can be life-savers, especially if you are a long way away from home:
• Thermos of hot drink
• Biscuits
• Toilet roll
• Gloves
• An assistant!

Small pots of summer flowers can come in handy for adding colour to large floral decorations.

• Twine and raffia
• Stem-binding or gutta-percha tape: looks like a flower or plant stem and helps to seal in moisture
• Tissue paper: for boxing and supporting finished arrangements
• Water sprayer to keep things moist when finished
• Hammer: to crush the end of woody stemmed materials
• Secateurs and scissors: I only use scissors, but my hands have become strong enough to cut most stems. You may need secateurs to cut woody stems.
• Sharp knife
• Pins: pearl headed and plain for attaching buttonholes.

Basic Techniques

Wiring Flowers

One of the most difficult yet important techniques to master when working with flowers is that of wiring. Some flowers and foliage must be wired if they are to be used in certain ways. The wiring of single flowers, leaves and florets is different to that needed for bunches of heads and groups of foliage, etc, to use in garlands and larger designs.

I remember trying so hard to learn how to wire something properly, but always the wire either remained too loose around the stems or cut through them and everything fell apart. Then suddenly, something clicked and at last I was able to 'wire up', as professionals call it.

So be patient and persistent, and after a little practice you too will be able to make up all manner of ambitious designs with a professional floral-decorator's flair.

The method of wiring explained here is known as a double-leg mount.

~ 1 ~

Take 3–5 flower heads and arrange them in your hand until you are satisfied with their position, bearing in mind the use to which they will be put. Cut the stems about 7.5–10cm (3–4in) long.

~ 2 ~

Take a 30cm (12in) stub wire and form a hairpin shape. Hold the loop over the flower stems with your thumb.

~ 3 ~

Bend one end of the wire over and
around the stems, binding them securely
but not too tightly to the other wire.
Wind the wire around the stems three or
four times.

~ 4 ~

The flowers should be securely held on
the wire and you should be left with two
lengths of wire, protruding below the
flower(s). These will be used to attach
the flowers into your chosen base.

Wiring Fruit

All manner and variety of fruits – and
even vegetables – can be wired in a very
similar way to flowers, above, by piercing
them with wire and making it into a
double-leg mount. The piercing is
necessary to support the weight of the
fruit or vegetable.

Pierce the object with the wire itself,
draw it through and bend the two ends
down to form a large hairpin. Twist one
wire onto the other to make it secure. You
are left with the wires protruding below
the wired item.

Basic Moss Bases

Moss bases are used in floral arrangements to provide a firm, moisture-retentive base on which to work. The moss usually used is spagnum moss, also known as sack moss. It is more flexible and less messy than the water-retaining foam (most commonly known as Oasis). Flowers can be wired into dampened moss and still be able to take up moisture while they are attached.

Moss is used either bound with reel wire, or

~ 1 ~

Cut the required length of 30cm (12in)-wide 5cm (2in)-mesh chicken wire, and allow an extra 5cm (2in) each end to tuck in. Bend up the 'selvedge' sides to form a trough. Fill with damp moss which has been teased out to remove any foreign bodies. Push the moss down to form a depth of 5–7.5cm (2–3in).

~ 2 ~

Bring the opposite side of the mesh down onto the moss, pressing it down quite firmly. Make cuts along the selvedge of the wire on the remaining upright side, at 5cm (2in) intervals. Push this side of wire down onto the moss/wire surface. You have now in effect created a moss and chicken-wire sandwich. Using the short length of wire created from cutting the selvedge, secure the second edge to the wire of the base. Press down firmly to create a flat base. Fold in each end, and secure as above.

held within a frame of chicken wire. It is also useful as a packing material to ensure pots fit snugly within larger containers.

Moss often needs to be checked over before use in order to remove any lumps of root, soil or other foreign bodies. If not removed, these might later get in the way while the flowers are being inserted.

The instructions below show you how to make a moss base for a garland, swag or drop.

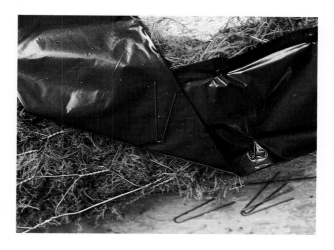

~ 3 ~

Cut a piece of thick black polythene, at least as long as the finished base, and slightly narrower than the finished width. Lay it on the surface of the moss and chicken wire. Secure at intervals with short stub wires. These should pierce the polythene and secure it into the moss. Once complete, turn the base over. You now have a length of moss base which will provide sufficient moisture to maintain the plant material in it, and yet will not damage the surface against which it is to be hung.

~ 4 ~

Wire small bunches of foliage and flowers, as shown on pages 18–19. Push these into the front of the garland, and allow the wire ends to pierce the polythene and come out onto the back. Bend the wire ends back into the base, thus securing the wired bunch and leaving no sharp wires on the back of the garland. Flowers, fruits, baskets and pots etc can all be added in a similar way.

Wedding One
A COUNTRY CHURCH

St John's Church, Stoke Clandon, Somerset

IT IS WITH TREPIDATION THAT I MAKE A FIRST VISIT to a church with the bride or her mother, for often it is the style and setting of the church that will immediately decide the feel of the wedding and its flowers.

However, there is nothing more wonderful than arriving at a beautiful country church with glorious architectural features just crying out to be decorated. Do let your imagination run riot, but be warned that before you decide on your final decorative scheme, the views of the vicar or the churchwardens must be consulted, and their permission given.

Here I would like to make a gentle plea for tolerance on all sides. Generally, the church authorities fall into two camps. There are the 'glad you are here' groups, and the 'Oh, you are from London, are you!' groups. The former are a joy to know, pleased to see their church being enjoyed and glorified, and are usually as excited and enthusiastic about the whole affair as the bride. The latter seem full of resentment at the use of their building by outsiders, and it can be a constant battle between the two interested parties, which seems sad, as generally the end result is one which looks wonderful and makes the bride's and groom's special day one for everyone to remember.

Once you have decided on your decorations, you must also work out the basic essentials. Is water freely available? How far away is the tap? Will you need a hosepipe? Who holds the key to the church, and what time is it locked or unlocked? It is advisable to contact the person responsible for the church's flowers to ascertain

A country corsage of delphiniums, pink spray roses and feverfew. It would look equally charming, made a little larger, as a posy for a young bridesmaid.

whether or not there are any other services taking place when you wish to decorate the church. You should also find out if the flowers are to be left in the church, and when it would be convenient to return and collect your containers, etc.

Do not forget that working in a church can be tiring and cold, so take a thick sweater and some food with you. And do not forget to take the necessities for cleaning up, such as rubbish (trash) bags, dust sheets, a broom and a dustpan and brush.

Working out the order in which to do the flowers is very important as a church is generally cooler than the reception rooms. Therefore, if you are able to arrange the church flowers ahead of time it

Marguerite daisies and feverfew give a typical 'English country' look.

will mean you have less of a last-minute rush to make sure everything gets done. However, flowers outside the church are ideally done on the day, as the wind and weather can take its toll. Be sure to bear all of this in mind when considering different types of floral decoration. Too much last-minute work can result in poor workmanship and frayed nerves.

Posy Pew Ends

Wedding flowers in a church should make an impact, and decorating the pew ends is an ideal way to ensure your flowers are seen and to create the feel of a church full of flowers. Pew ends appear to fill space and they create a focus for the bridal party as they move down the aisle.

Before deciding on pew ends, it is advisable to check first with the church's vicar. Some object to the pews being decorated as they are concerned about scratches or damage to the wood.

For a pew end of some size – which means you need a fairly wide aisle – an Oasis-based arrangement is best. Remember that these displays are going to hang vertically, so make sure that all you add is firmly held by the Oasis.

Attach your pew end with wire, looping it through the hole in the end of the handle and either hooking it over the top of the end of the wooden pew, or around the top of it. Never use nails, pins or sticky tape without the express permission of the church's vicar or churchwarden. Use ribbon or raffia, as here, to disguise the wire.

There is a particularly memorable scene in *Four Weddings and a Funeral* when Hugh Grant's character, Charles, arrives late for the wedding where he is to be best man. He quickly picks a stem of Doris pink from a pew end in the church and puts it into his buttonhole. With almost all films nothing is ever filmed sequentially and various shots were 'picked up' throughout the six-week shoot. This meant that wherever I went throughout the filming I had to ensure there was a regular supply of pinks for Charles' buttonhole.

WHAT YOU WILL NEED

FOR EACH PEW END • ¹/₃ block Oasis (see page 16) • Oasis spade • Oasis tape, green if possible
Stub wires • 3 short stems variegated pittosporum foliage • 3 stems *Viburnum tinus* • 2–3 stems *Senecio greyi*
3–4 stems silver-leafed plant • 7 stems antirrhinum (snapdragon) • 5 stems phlox
3 stems 'Blue Bees' delphinium • 3 stems white daisy chrysanthemum • 10 stems 'Bridal Pink' rose
7 stems 'Eskimo White' rose • 5 stems pink spray rose

~ 1 ~

This Oasis-based arrangement can be done at home, along with table decorations, etc, and taken to the church on the day before the wedding. Using an Oasis spade, cut a block of Oasis to the correct size. Soak it and push it firmly into the spade. Tape it securely in two places, as in the picture. Avoid taping across the centre of the block as the tape would get in the way once it comes to adding the flowers and foliage.

~ 2 ~

With the spade handle at the top (ie, at 12 noon) cover the Oasis with the foliage, working with one type at a time. Use the viburnum first to establish the shape, which should be a rough circle. Do not forget to cut and split any hard or woody stems as you push them in. Avoid becoming too carried away with foliage; use it to cover the mechanics and allow it to act as a foil for the flowers, which are the star performers. Too much foliage will result in a heavy looking pew end to which it will be difficult to add flowers.

~ 3 ~

Add the chrysanthemum sprays. You should be able to cut each stem of chrysanthemum into about three pieces, some with buds, others all open blooms. Use the blooms first, recessing them slightly. Use the budded stems towards the outside edge. Next put in the antirrhinums, again following the outside edge. They will have to be cut quite short to prevent them protruding too much in a spiky manner. Use one or two even shorter and put them in towards the centre of the design, but avoid putting one right in the middle as it will protrude too much once the complete arrangement is hanging up.

Add the phlox, leaving them slightly larger than the chrysanthemums as they are lighter flowers. Distribute all the flowers throughout the design to achieve the effect of an informal posy.

~ 4 ~

Now add the roses, both pink and white. Some of them should be left longer, others placed in deeper, to give depth of colour. As you have plenty of pink roses, you can create a slightly clumped effect by grouping them in twos and threes.

Finally, add the spray roses and the stem of delphinium, both of which may be broken down into several stems with a few flower heads on each. Leave the roses at the edges slightly longer to create a loose effect.

Until you become practised, it may be useful to hang up each pew end as you finish it, just to check that it is uniform in shape and everything sits well within the design. Do not leave it hanging until you can put it into the church, however, as the water will drain to the bottom of the Oasis, leaving some parts quite dry.

Tied-bunch Bouquet

*This most elegant yet simple bridal bouquet contains a variety of both flowers and foliage.
For a country wedding, or a celebration that is not particularly formal, it may not seem
appropriate for a bride to carry a structured bouquet of wired flowers and foliage.
Some bridal gowns need an ornate bouquet, but other less formal dresses may look
far more effective teamed with a simple tied bouquet.*

As the first wedding in the film was a country wedding we wanted to have a relaxed bouquet, full of late spring and early summer flowers. Due to the length of time that filming takes, and the problem of continuity, I arranged the bride's bouquet in a special bridal holder: a plastic handle holding a small sphere of water-retentive foam into which the flowers are inserted. The effect is nearly the same as the bouquet described here, and the flowers are still able to drink. Even so, I don't like these devices and would never use them for a real wedding because I would not feel confident that the flowers were secure or stable enough.

In the film, the bouquet is thrown to the remaining guests as the happy couple leave for their honeymoon. The filming took place at 1 o'clock in the morning. Unfortunately, the bridesmaid was not good at catching and the bouquet was crushed every time, so I still flinch when remembering the number of bouquets I had to make over and over again.

WHAT YOU WILL NEED
FOR ONE BOUQUET • 3–4 stems *Viburnum tinus* • 3 stems *Helleborus foetidus* • 3 stems *Vinca major*
2 short stems guelder rose (*Viburnum opulus*) • 2–3 stems silver-leafed plant • 2 stems *Senecio greyi*
2 stems variegated pittosporum • 5 stems antirrhinum (snapdragon) • 2 stems 'Blue Bees' delphinium
3 stems white daisy chrysanthemum • 1 stem September flower ('Monte Carlo' chrysanthemum)
3 stems phlox • 2 stems pink spray rose • 10 stems 'Bridal Pink' rose • 3 stems 'Eskimo White' rose
Raffia or twine • Co-ordinating ribbon

~ 1 ~

Begin by sorting and conditioning all the different foliage and flowers. You will require quite a large working surface to allow you to spread out each type of plant material, without crowding it and damaging delicate blooms. Carefully clean all the lower leaves and thorns, etc, from the stems. Do not scar the stems or leave behind any thorns which may prick the hands or damage expensive wedding clothes – especially the bride's dress.

It is essential to prepare all the foliage and flowers before you begin to make up the bouquet, because once it is started you will need both hands to construct the bouquet: one to hold the arrangement, and the other to add new material.

~ 2 ~

Arrange the foliage first, working with one type of material at a time.

Using one hand as a 'vase' loosely hold the stems as you arrange them to your satisfaction. Start with the viburnum as a base, using it slightly recessed so that the strong dark leaves will act as a support for the other material, both physically and visually. Then add the silvered and variegated foliage in prominent positions, to take full advantage of their interesting colouring.

~ 3 ~

When you have created a pleasing shape with the foliage, add the flowers (except the roses), one type at a time, using antirrhinum and delphinium first. Add the stems of guelder rose as you go, recessing some to create depth.

As you work, each stem should twist around one position from the last, so that eventually you end up with the stems all forming a spiral shape. When adding each stem, place it across the bunch, secure it with the other hand, then turn the bunch a few degrees, add another stem, secure with the hand and rotate again. Gradually you will build up your bouquet into a pleasing and regular rounded shape.

~ 4 ~

The last flowers to add are the beautiful pink roses. These are pushed into the posy from above while holding it in your hand. This ensures that they will be prominent and will not have been crushed by the other flowers as the bouquet was being composed.

A frill of citrus green hellebore around the outside edge helps to cover the hand slightly and sets off the fresh colours of the flowers. Once the bouquet is complete, tie it off with either twine or raffia, and stand in a bucket of water.

Thirty minutes before the bouquet is required, take it out of the water and using a towel, pat dry the stem ends. Tie a ribbon around it forming a discreet bow. The bouquet is now ready to be carried by the bride.

Bridesmaid's Flower Ball

Flower balls have been a great wedding favourite for many years, and look particularly attractive when carried by younger bridesmaids. They are an excellent project for the inexperienced flower arranger, who otherwise may find the idea of arranging flowers for three or four bridesmaids rather daunting. Flower balls are relatively quick to make and become easier with practice.

Flower balls are often called pomanders, though they bear little resemblance to the dried fruit studded with cloves which Elizabethan women carried to ward off unpleasant smells.

However, they do retain the rounded shape of the fruit at the centre in the form of a purchased Oasis sphere, which makes the balls relatively easy to put together.

While the shape of these balls is visually very pleasing, and can provide a charming alternative to a more traditional bouquet, do be warned: I have lost count of the weddings I have attended where young bridesmaids have used their flower balls as giant conkers (chestnuts). It may look comical and fun, but it does the flowers no good whatsoever.

If you arrange the ball the night before it is to be used, the well-soaked Oasis sphere does not need to be covered in polythene. Any water that may drip out of it will stop within a short time of completing the ball.

WHAT YOU WILL NEED

FOR EACH BALL • 1 sphere Oasis, 10cm (4in) diameter • Raffia or string • 30cm (12in) stub wire
Silver wire • 60 heads ranunculus in two colours, at various stages of opening
2 stems 'Blue Bees' dephinium, with side shoots
1 stem September flower ('Monte Carlo' chrysanthemum) • 3–5 stems *Helleborus foetidus*
2 stems pink spray roses • In place of the ranunculus it would be possible to use
grape hyacinths, roses, violets, Doris pinks or even spray carnations. Lily of the valley could be
substituted for the helleborus.

~ 1 ~

Before the invention of Oasis and other water-retaining materials, a ball of damp moss was used as a base. This meant that all the flowers had to be wired before they could be assembled. Thankfully, we are now able to use Oasis, thus avoiding the need to wire many of the flowers. Soak the sphere thoroughly before starting to work.

Take 30cm (12in) of stub wire and bend it in half to form a long hairpin shape. Put the wire through the centre of the ball. Wrap the free ends of the wire round a tough 2.5cm (1in) piece of stem, and pull the loop up so the stem rests tightly against the Oasis. This should prevent the wire cutting through the ball. Attach a piece of string or raffia to the loop to use as a handle while assembling the ball.

~ 2 ~

Cut the ranunculus heads on the slant, leaving about 3.5cm (1^1/2in) of stem to push into the Oasis. Insert all the heads, working them quite closely together, incorporating a variety of sizes and colours. Try to clump the colours rather than alternating them. This can result in a somewhat dotted effect which would look rather contrived.

You may find it helpful to rest the ball on a pillow of crumpled tissue paper to prevent damaging the flower heads as you begin to cover the whole sphere. It is also possible to suspend the ball from a door frame or chair back while you are working on it, although it can tend to spin round which may be annoying.

~ 3 ~

Having covered most of the sphere, a
small gap will remain at the upper,
looped end of the ball. Take single florets
of 'Blue Bees' delphinium and mount
them on to silver wire (see pages 18–19).
Once the delphinium is wired up, place it
in the gaps between the ranunculus
heads, again in a random fashion.

~ 4 ~

At the top (loop) end of the ball, replace
the string or raffia work-handle with a
loop of fine ribbon, or a bold raffia
handle which has been bound at intervals
to ensure it fits comfortably into a child's
small hand.

To fill the narrow gap around the wire
loop, make up a little 'top-knot' using
small side-shoots of delphinium and
sprigs of September flower. Add some
spray roses or tiny rosebuds, making sure
that the stems go well into the Oasis and
are secure. Do not cut them too long as
they may be in the way when the ball is
being carried. A few heads of citrus green
hellebore will finish off this dainty
flower ball.

Spray with a fine mist, hang it up so none
of the heads get damaged, and cover
with damp tissue paper until needed.

Lych Gate

This lovely arch will be admired by all your wedding guests as they pass through it on the way in and out of the church, and will provide a delightful frame for the wedding photographs that will be treasured for many years to come.

A church gate such as this is an ideal place to create a real statement.

As it is such a rural setting, the stone and brick walls were an excellent foil for the use of old baskets and terracotta pots, filled with a selection of glorious early summer blooms. What could

be more natural than Victorian terracotta pots of flowers sitting on the wall? These include clear blue forget-me-nots, or as a small friend of mine, Ruari Cannon, calls them: 'remember-mes'.

A gate like this was made especially for the film, but unfortunately you never really see it – a great shame when you consider the amount of work involved. It was at this time that the weather suddenly turned very hot. The cast and extras had to wear their wedding garb all day long, and soon people were dropping like flies as they fainted in the unaccustomed heat.

A gate like this can be a problem in extremes of weather – be it particularly hot or cold – so it may not be advisable to attempt it if very hot weather is forecast. If it does get particularly hot, the young tips of ivy and other foliage should be snipped off if they look in fear of wilting, and as many flowers as possible should be used in extension tubes to allow them to continue drinking while in the arrangement.

WHAT YOU WILL NEED

FOR GATE SIMILAR TO SIZE IN PHOTOGRAPH • 100 stems long trailing ivy • 75 stems leather-leaf fern
30 stems *Senecio greyi* • 24 x 7.5cm (3in)-wide plastic pots mixed short foliage plants
(such as scented geranium, trailing grey helichrysum) • 25 white daisy chrysanthemum
100 stems blue Canterbury bells • 100 stems pink Canterbury bells • 100 stems mixed stock
60 stems short guelder rose (*Viburnum opulus*) • 150 stems pink spray roses
Selection of flowering plants in terracotta pots (Victorian if possible)

~ 1 ~

Make a moss base, or a series of bases, in
a chicken-wire frame (see pages 20–21).
There is no need to put the polythene on
the back of the base when it is being used
outdoors in such a setting. Only use a
polythene backing if there is a danger of
scratching or wetting something delicate
or valuable.

Firmly attach the base to the archway or
gate, using galvanized wire. Make sure
the moss covers all the sides of the
gateway so that there is no bare metal or
wood showing.

~ 2 ~

Wire up all the lengths of trailing ivy,
and attach them to the arch to cover as
much of the mossed base as possible.
Remember to work all sides of the base,
from the top to the ground.

Add stems of leather-leaf fern and
senecio until your base is virtually
covered all around.

~ 3 ~

Next, add all the plastic pots of
helichrysum and small scented-leaf
geraniums. First, each one must be wired
up with a large double-leg mount (see
pages 18–19). Push a 45cm (18in)-long
18 gauge wire through the bottom hole
of the pot, bend the wire over at the top,
and bring it down the outside of the pot
to form a double-leg mount at the base.
Use this wire to attach the pots to the
moss. Add them in clumps of two or
three pots to create an effect as if they
are growing. Space the groups 15–30cm
(6–12in) apart throughout.

~ 4 ~

Stems of white daisy chrysanthemum,
blue and pink Canterbury bells are next
added to the garland.

If they have been well conditioned in
water beforehand (for several days) they
should last in the garland, obtaining their
moisture merely from the moss. You may
find it necessary to secure some of them
using stub wires.

Again, work through the whole arch.

~5~

Some flowers need to drink constantly or they will wither in a very short time, so they are placed in plastic extension tubes before being added to the display (see page 17). In this way mixed stocks and guelder rose are incorporated.

By now the decoration is almost complete. Any large remaining gaps can be filled with extra foliage or handfuls of green moss.

~6~

The last flowers to be added are the pink spray roses. These are made up into bunches, with three to five stems per bunch. This is to ensure that they do not get lost in the large arrangement, and make a small impact in their own right. Again, because they need a considerable amount of water, they are placed in extension tubes to ensure they remain as fresh as possible.

~7~

To maintain the country feel, the Victorian terracotta pots have been placed around the base of the gate and on the walls at the side. These are planted with a variety of typically English cottage-garden flowers such as thrift, campanula, scented geraniums and forget-me-nots. They help to anchor the design of the gateway by tying it into the wall, and providing extra flowering bulk at each side of the base.

~8~

The finished arch. To keep it fresh for as long as possible it can be given a thorough spray with a fine mist of water. However, it is advisable not to do this just as the bride is about to arrive, as it would be disastrous to get water, pollen or smears on the bridal dress.

NEXT PAGE A floral garland, made from a rope of wired foliage and flowers, and an unusual flower 'tree' are ideal decorations for a country wedding reception.

Flower Tree

This delightfully decorative and imposing 'tree' uses a variety of country-style flowers to continue your chosen floral scheme at the wedding reception. It is an ideal size to make an impact at a large venue, or in a garden, while using only a relatively small quantity of flowers.

For large marquees, big reception rooms or buffet tables, where some height is needed in an arrangement, a flower tree is often an ideal solution. It allows you to make a sizeable decoration which can be clearly seen, yet it does not take up too much of the table space, nor does it obstuct people's views as they talk down the table.

This example is an ingenious construction that is easy to put together yourself, given sufficient practicality and advance planning. A wooden 'trunk' is made from a pole of birch (available from large garden centres). Birch has an attractive silvery bark that needs no additional decoration.

The most important thing to ensure is that the tree is well supported and stable, in a pot to prevent it falling over. It is wise to secure the trunk in the pot with plaster or cement, making the pot as heavy as possible.

A framework is added at the top, on which to build the ball of flowers. This is constructed from a wire hanging basket, blocks of Oasis and a framework of chicken-wire mesh.

The decorative effect is completed by covering the pot at the bottom with a neat, green trim, made from green bamboo held in place with a rope of raffia, finished off with green carpet moss.

WHAT YOU WILL NEED

FOR ONE FLOWER TREE • 1–1.2m (3¹/2–4ft) birch pole, about 10cm(4in) diameter • Plastic pot
Cement or plaster • 25–30cm (10–12in) diameter circular wire hanging basket • Large metal staples
Hammer • 5–6 Oasis blocks (see page 16) • Chicken wire • Phlox • Marguerite • Delphinium • Aquilegia
Blown heads of roses • Ranunculus • Double pale pink *Eustoma grandiflorum* • White roses • Feverfew
Heavy straight-sided terracotta pot • Snake grass or green bamboo • Reel wire • Raffia
Moss • Green carpet moss

~ 1 ~

Set the birch pole firmly into the pot.

Cut the bottom out of a wire hanging basket and push it on to the pole, leaving 15cm (6in) of pole protruding into the basket. Secure it to the pole using the staples and a hammer. Cover the basket with chicken wire and fill with Oasis blocks. Cover them with another piece of mesh, securing it to the basket's rim.

Select short, bulky pieces of foliage (approximately 15cm (6in) long), for covering your Oasis. You are only really using them to cover the Oasis, as the flowers will protrude above the foliage.

~ 2 ~

Start adding the flowers. Stems of phlox and marguerite have good foliage which will help to cover the Oasis, and they are quite dense, helping to fill in the shape while still looking relatively light. The delphinium has been cut into short lengths and added in clumps of three or five stems at a time to form patches of blue without protruding too much. The daintiness of the aquilegia helps to lift the whole design.

~ 3 ~

Working the whole at one go, add the rest of the flowers type by type. Blown heads of roses and ranunculus are wonderful because they create strong areas of colour and fill in quite quickly. I have also used double pale pink *E.grandiflorum*, which looks as if it was made from tulle it is so dainty. White roses and feverfew are also used to lift the design. Once you have filled the whole of the top, put it to one side.

~ 4 ~

Wrap the sides of the terracotta pot with snake grass or green bamboo. It is fiddly, requiring either two pairs of hands or lots of reel wire: attach a wire around the pot and carefully bind on handfuls of snake grass, binding around the whole pot as you go. Keep the binding point of the wire in the middle of the pot.

Once the pot is covered, make a wide band of raffia to cover the wire. Place the tree inside the pot, packing it firmly with wet moss to prevent it from moving about. Cover the top with sheets of fresh green carpet moss.

Garland of Flowers and Foliage

The graceful, curving shape of a length of garland adds a pretty detail that lends itself beautifully to a country setting. This sort of decoration could be used at either the church or the reception, but it is particularly ideal for decorating the table for the buffet, bridal party or wedding cake. Its gentle but arresting shape will irresistably focus the attention of all your guests on the most important areas of the celebration.

For a light garland or rope of flowers that is suitable for decorating the front of a table, it isn't necessary to use a moss base. The garland is made from a base of greenery wired into a rope, with flowers bound on to it, making a length of decoration that is flexible enough to fall into the graceful curving shape required.

Not using moss, however, means that flowers are not able to drink once they are added to the garland. As a result, it can only be made up at the last minute, as close to the time of use as possible.

To attach the garland to a clothed table first pin a 30cm (12in) stub wire on to the cloth, at the upper points from which the garland is to hang (near the top edge of the table). Using at least two or three long pins, attach the middle of the wire to the cloth. Thread one end of the wire through the end of the garland from back to front. Twist that end with the other end of the wire, and poke the ends back into the garland so they are hidden.

You may wish to add a bow of ribbon or raffia, or a small tied bunch of flowers, to decorate the ends of the garland.

WHAT YOU WILL NEED
FOR A 1.2M (4FT) LENGTH OF GARLAND • 30 stems trailing ivy • Variety of short foliage
(such as ming fern, pittosporum, etc in 13–15cm (5–6in) pieces) • 15 stems flowering marguerite
5 stems 'Blue Bees' delphinium • 10 stems pink phlox • 30 heads blown pink ranunculus
20 stems 'Bridal Pink' rose • 20 stems 'Eskimo White' rose • 20 stems double pink *Eustoma grandiflorum*
40 stems mixed aquilegia • Reel wire

~ 1 ~

Begin by cutting all the flowers into short lengths and sorting them into types. The roses should be de-thorned and most of the foliage must be removed. This will enable you to begin the garland and assemble it in total without having to break off to prepare more flowers.

Take five stems of ivy and bind them together with the reel wire. The ivy will now act as your base in place of moss. On to this ivy base attach a couple of stems of pittosporum.

~ 2 ~

Add three stems of marguerite, and attach using the reel wire. Next add some roses and bind again.

As you work, add in more stems of ivy to maintain a solid base and cover up the binding wire.

~ 3 ~

As you work down the garland ensure
you are using a good variety of your
available flowers. Make sure the flowers
are added randomly, but that a regular
shape is achieved. Therefore it is
essential that the delphinium are cut
down into shorter clumps, to prevent
them sticking out too much.

You will find the base becomes quite firm
as the stems of the previous bunch act as
support for the subsequent flowers that
are wired in.

~ 4 ~

Finish off using some attractive trails of
ivy at the end. You may also find it
necessary to wire three to five heads of
rose (see pages 18–19), to cover the
point where you finish off your wiring.

When the garland is finished, spray
lightly, box down, cover with wet tissue
and put to one side until required.

Wedding Two

TOTALLY TRADITIONAL

St Julian's, Smithfield, London EC1

THE MARRIAGE OF BERNARD TO LYDIA IN *FOUR WEDDINGS* was the most conventional-looking of all and thus the style of arrangements I created was fairly standard – the sort of things one might be asked to create for many weddings throughout the season.

Certainly, the most popular colourings for wedding decorations in England are still pale pastel shades, teamed with whites, creams, and various shades of green. Many people still feel that a typical summer wedding should have young bridesmaids dressed in pale frocks and page boys in sailor suits. Even so, this need not be the case and you can easily use pale colours with dramatic and unusual hues. The essential aim is to pin down exactly what the bride herself would like to have – the type of 'look' she is aiming for, whether conventional or unusual, understated or dramatic. It is then up to the floral decorator to design the bouquet, church flowers or reception decorations to achieve precisely that effect.

The flowers I have used here are old favourites: lilies, roses, sweet peas and ivy, but teamed up with a collection of California poppies, paeonies and fritillaria for an unusual finish. Traditional baskets are used, together with modern glass-tank containers and rough terracotta candle pots. All of this eclectic mix can work well if carefully planned and executed. I think nothing looks more wonderful than a pure white cloth, immaculately ironed and set with simple silver cutlery, glass and china, with an uncomplicated but beautiful mixture of summer flowers in a rustic basket. The traditional theme is carried through to the napkins which have been bound with green twine, to which is attached a tiny posy of scented thyme and cream sweet peas. What a wonderful welcome for your guests as they sit down to enjoy the wedding breakfast.

The flowers for the bridal party could not be more traditional.

Tiny posies of cream sweet peas and dark green thyme bound together make fragrant table-napkin decorations. They look beautiful in combination with the Table Decoration described on pages 66-69.

Sweet peas, poppies, pink roses, and sweetly drooping dicentra are an idyllic combination of summer flowers.

White lilac and roses, freesias and lily of the valley form a stunning bridal headdress, but with the addition of tiny wired seed pearls to add a sparkle. The result is quite magical.

Simplicity is essential for the most effective results when using such glorious materials. For example, a small selection of lilies, roses and sweet peas is used to decorate an eighteenth-century candlestick which stands near the entrance to our beautiful church. The uncluttered lines of the architecture match perfectly with the uncomplicated decoration.

Whatever you choose to do, by ensuring the flowers are presented in a simple and uncluttered way, you are bound to create an effective and beautiful display. As well as being enjoyed by your guests, the decorations will provide a superb and memorable background for the bride's big day.

House Flowers

There is nothing more welcoming to your wedding guests than a fresh vase of flowers. Here, a delightfully subtle combination of poppies and sweet peas makes up a charming but discreet decoration for any room of the home.

If you are planning a wedding or party at home, try to remember to plan for at least a couple of floral arrangements, but if you are expecting a large number of people, do not make the flowers too large or they may get in the way, and could, unfortunately, even be knocked over.

The container for this collection of flowers is a simple rectangular glass tank. Start with it half full of clean water. This type of decoration is intended to look informal and unarranged, so it is not essential to use masses of one or two types of flower, and the shape of the finished arrangement, although quite ordered, should not be contained and rigid.

It is always advisable to arrange home flowers *in situ* to ensure that they are compatible with their surroundings and the decor of the room in which they are to reside.

When the flowers have been arranged, top up the water level in the glass container to within an inch of the top. Although you will no doubt become extremely busy, ensure it is kept well topped up, especially within the first 24 hours when the flowers will take up large quantities of water.

It is very important, with a clear container, to keep the water as clean as possible so that the arrangement looks fresh and attractive.

WHAT YOU WILL NEED

23cm (9in)-square glass tank • 12 stems euphorbia • 5 stems pale pink campanula • 5 stems fritillaria
20 stems California poppy • 3 stems cream antirrhinum (snapdragon)• 5 stems pale blue delphinium
20 stems mauve sweet pea • 20 stems cream sweet pea • 5 stems pale pink 'Sarah Bernhardt' paeony
3 stems pink spray rose • 3 stems 'Vanilla' rose • 3 stems bleeding heart (*Dicentra spectabilis*)
10 stems bear grass

~ 1 ~

Begin by arranging the foliage.
Remember to strip the foliage from the
lower parts of all the stems – both foliage
and flowers – to prevent them rotting
and turning the water sour.

Stems of euphorbia and campanula are
cut, split and placed in the tank with the
shorter stems to the sides. As always,
work with one type of material at a time.

~ 2 ~

California poppies are added next. These
soft stems are much happier in plain
water than Oasis, and so are ideal for this
style of decoration.

Antirrhinum and delphinium flowers are
crucial to create some height, and the
beautiful black fritillaria gives wonderful
silhouettes to the design.

~ 3 ~

Several bunches of pastel-coloured sweet peas help to fill out the design but do not look heavy or overpowering.

It would be quite acceptable to leave the arrangement at this stage. Although it has no floral focus it still looks charming.

~ 4 ~

Beautiful blown heads of 'Sandra Bernhardt' paeonies, some dainty dicentra and some strap-like foliage complete the design. The paeonies give focal interest and by using just three you are able to see the perfection of these flowers without overcrowding the surrounding material.

NEXT PAGE *Often, the simplest of flowers are the most beautiful, and in the same way uncomplicated arrangements can have the most wonderful effect. Here, a beautiful eighteenth-century wooden candlestick looks stunning with a group of pale pastel-shaded lilies, roses and sweet peas surrounding a thick beeswax candle. The flowers are supported by blocks of Oasis, wrapped in chicken wire and attached to the central pole. The soft colour of the stone walls and flowers are the perfect foil for such a design. At the side is a posy of roses, lilies and euphorbia.*

Bride's Headdress

A bridal circlet of perfect lily of the valley, scented freesia and stephanotis is complemented by small dark ivy leaves and a sprinkling of seed pearls. This is often one of the last things to be made as it will wilt quite quickly, but it is very fiddly to make so plenty of time must be allowed. Discuss the bride's veil and hairstyle in advance so that your circlet will be just right on the day, as there will be little time available then to rectify any problems.

WHAT YOU WILL NEED

40 stems lily of the valley • 20–30 small dark ivy leaves • 1 bag (20 heads) stephanotis
10 stems white freesia • 5 stems white lilac • 50 seed pearls attached to silver wire • Silver reel wire
Silver rose wire • 18-gauge stub wires • Green stem-binding tape

~ 1 ~

Measure the bride's head and make up a
ring to fit from stub wire. Cover with
stem-binding tape.

The stems of lily of the valley have a
silver rose wire wound down them from
tip to toe to ensure that they do not wilt.
This is possibly one of the most fiddly of
all floristry tasks and requires great
patience and dexterity. When you order
the lily of the valley, be prepared for a
few damaged stems and order some extra
to compensate.

~ 2 ~

Take perfect, single ivy leaves. Pierce the
back of each leaf with a silver wire, as if
taking a tiny stitch across the central
vein. Then bend the wires down to form
a hairpin shape. Bind one wire around
the other, trapping and securing the
stem-end as you bind. This will provide
support for the leaf and allow you to
bend it into the desired shape.

~ 3 ~

Individual florets of stephanotis, freesia
and lilac, together with the ivy leaves
and lily of the valley, are bound on to the
ring of wire which forms the base of the
headdress. I have also used seed pearls on
little wires to add a touch of glamour and
sparkle to the finished design.

As each item is positioned on the circlet,
bind it with one or two turns of silver
reel wire to ensure it is secure and cannot
slip. Then snip off the wired 'stem' of the
leaf or flower you have just added, just
beyond the binding wire. This prevents a
build up of bulky wires which could
make the headdress heavy and
uncomfortable to wear.

~ 4 ~

You can see how the pearls add a
shimmer to the finished design. Do not
worry about the silver binding wire on
the inside of the circlet as once it is in
place, the bride's hair and/or the veil will
cover all the wires.

When the circlet is complete, lay it on
damp tissue, cover with more tissue and
put away carefully until it is required.

Table Decoration

For a relaxed and appealing reception-table centre there is nothing more appropriate than a collection of beautiful high-summer flowers. Here, California poppies, sweet peas and spray roses have been combined in an arrangement that is fresh, subtle and interesting.

Before starting to plan a table-centre arrangement, find out both the size and shape of the tables to be decorated, as this is bound to affect the style and size of arrangement required.

Be bold and ensure the flowers are full and gutsy, but don't make them so large that they begin to get in everyone's way. There is nothing more maddening at a formal meal than having to fight through the flowers to find your cutlery, napkin or the salt and pepper.

It is not always easy to find a large number of attractive, low containers for table-centre arrangements. Therefore, I have suggested that for each you use a basket on the exterior, with a plastic bowl that fits snugly inside to hold the water and a ball of chicken-wire mesh. The plastic bowl can be firmly wedged inside the basket with moss.

When selecting your basket try, if possible, to find one without handles, as it may be difficult to insert your flowers around them while also maintaining the symmetry of the arrangement. As well, try to find a basket with a generous base, to ensure that the finished arrangement is stable.

As shown in the photograph, delightful additions include decorating the table-napkins with a small posy of sweet peas and fragrant thyme, and tiny scented nightlights in terracotta pots.

WHAT YOU WILL NEED

30cm (12in)-wide wicker basket • 25cm (10in)-wide plastic bowl to fit inside the basket • Moss
Polythene • Chicken wire (see page 16) • Reel wire • 10 stems euphorbia
10 dense and bushy 25cm (10in)-long stems rosemary • 15 stems California poppy
5 stems Bleeding heart (*Dicentra spectabilis*) • 20 stems mauve sweet pea • 20 stems cream sweet pea
5 stems 'Porcelain' spray rose • 5 stems pink spray rose

~ 1 ~

Put a loose ball of chicken wire (see page
16) into the plastic bowl, and using reel
wire go across the bottom of the bowl,
up each side and sew the reel wire into
the chicken wire. Line the basket with
polythene and then put the bowl into the
basket packing moss around the edges to
ensure it fits tightly. Make sure no moss
protrudes into the bowl as it will syphon
the water out. Fill the bowl two-thirds
full of clean water.

~ 2 ~

Work with one type of foliage at a time.
Cut a piece off, split its stem end (if hard
or woody) and push it through the wire
into the bowl ensuring its ends are well
into the water. Work from the edges of
the basket into the centre, making sure
the arrangement does not get too tall or
protrude too much at the sides. Try to
achieve a uniform outline with the
foliage to cover as much of the chicken
wire as possible.

Choosing one type of flower at a time,
put into the basket the more soft-
stemmed flowers. It will be easier to
place them now before the wire becomes
too crowded.

~ 3 ~

Continue to add the flowers. Any which
are naturally inclined to curve, such as
dicentra, are best placed around the
edges to help cover the sides of the bowl
and to break up the edge of the basket.

As you work, remember the finished
arrangement will be seen from a seated
position, so do not neglect the outer
edges, and make very sure the plastic
bowl will be hidden from sight.

~ 4 ~

Add the rest of your flowers to the
arrangement, all the time remembering
not to make it too tall. Position the roses
last to create focal interest and to fill in
any gaps. Ensure that all the stems are in
water, and keep the container topped up
until required.

Floral Chair Back

What more welcoming and wonderful sight could there be than to walk into a room filled with beautiful flowers, wonderful china, glass and silver, and to sit on a chair decorated with a garland of fragrant, fresh flowers?

A floral decoration attached to the back of a chair gives a delightful touch to any location. It may be that a marriage is to take place in a church, where traditional pews have been replaced by more ordinary chairs. Alternatively, floral chair backs may be particularly suitable for a registry-office wedding or, with the increasing tendency for marriages to take place in other locations, they could be the ideal way to introduce flowers into the proceedings.

At any wedding or grand affair the initial impact, followed by great attention to detail, is what people remember. Providing floral chair backs may seem extravagant – for indeed it is – but the impression your guests take away with them will last for many years.

You could always make a compromise and only decorate the ladies' chairs, or even just those for the top table or the guest of honour.

Because the flowers will be viewed close up as well as adding to the overall impact of the room, some of the flowers used here are quite delicate, such as the 'Golden Shower' orchids and the freesias.

All the flowers and foliage are bound on to a supporting base of a moss rope. This acts to hold them in place, to give shape to the overall design, and to provide the flowers with moisture so that they can last as long as the celebrations.

It is important to make sure, however, that the moss is only damp and not sodden, as a wet chair back could be distinctly uncomfortable.

WHAT YOU WILL NEED

Damp moss • Reel wire • Green carpet moss • 20 stems short green hebe • 5 stems solidaster
5 stems ming fern • 10 stems deep cream rose (wired individually) • 3 stems pink Cymbidium orchid
10 stems 'Golden Shower' spray orchid • 10 stems blown cream freesia

~ 1 ~

Make up a rope of damp moss by binding
it with reel wire to form a compact
sausage. Form a pair of loops from green
carpet moss, one at each end, to attach
the finished garland to the chair.

Working from each end to the centre
point, next bind on sprigs of foliage such
as hebe and ming fern, with pieces of
solidaster to give some colour. Cover the
moss quite roughly and work the back as
well as the front of the moss base. Bind
the foliage firmly, putting on one piece
of foliage then giving a turn of the wire
before adding the next piece. The piece
should not get too large or the finished
garland will become a nuisance once it is
in place.

Complete the 'greening up' of the
garland by finishing off the binding wire
in the middle.

~ 2 ~

Sprays of 'Golden Shower' orchids are
cut down into small bunches and wired
together. Those used at the ends of the
garland are left longer to allow some flow
at the sides, but those towards the
middle are kept shorter so that they do
not protrude too much.

Wire up individual stems of rose flowers
and push the wires into the moss, so that
they protrude from the back. Bend them
back into the moss to prevent any wires
from scratching the chair or its occupant.

~ 3 ~

In the same way, wire up small clumps of
blown cream freesia to fill in any gaps.

Ideally, the finished shape of the floral
decoration will be that of a smiling
mouth or a gently curved crescent, so try
to maintain this throughout.

~ 4 ~

Beautiful blush-pink heads of Cymbidum
orchid are wired individually and added
at the centre of the design, to provide a
focal point.

You can now hang the garland on the
back of the chair. Either leave it as it is,
or drape an unravelled flowering
stephanotis over it. This will soften the
whole effect of the arrangement and
provide some additional fragrance.

Wedding Three

A Scottish Chapel, by Night

The Chapel of Glenthrist Castle, Perthshire, Scotland

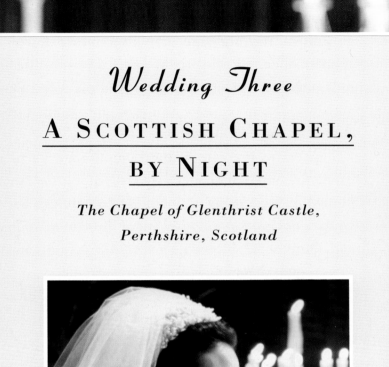

FOR A WINTER WEDDING, or for someone who wants something less traditional, the 'highland' style of wedding flowers illustrated in this chapter opens up all sorts of unusual possibilities. Rich purples and reds with deep cerise and pink are not the colours normally associated with weddings, yet they can look absolutely stunning if used with skill, flair and confidence.

Flowers in these rich, bold colours are particularly suited to a candlelit church or chapel, especially if it is on a small, intimate scale. However, huge pedestals of these colours can become dark holes if you are not careful, so be aware of the size of your venue, its lighting and the type of decorations required before you finally settle upon this colour scheme.

Warm colours and a bold style of decoration also go beautifully with tartan fabrics and furnishings, and can look stunning in a building where there is a preponderance of architectural features in stone, stained glass, dark woods and wrought iron. They also look extremely attractive in firelight.

Blue and purple anemones combined with strands of bear grass make an arresting 'highland-style' buttonhole (boutonniere). Make it up in the same way as the buttonholes described on pages 87-89.

The arrangements in the following pages make use of some unusual materials not always associated with weddings. For example, a variety of fruits and vegetables can look spectacular in decorations, especially when combined with dramatic reds, purples and blues. During the winter months, forced blooms of out-of-season flowers such as roses and lilies can be terribly expensive. It is often more economical to use fruits and vegetables to augment a selection of flowers, provided that all the elements in an arrangement are

carefully chosen to blend in with each other. Several of the displays that follow use fruit and vegetables, and there is no reason why you could not use any of these at either the reception or the church.

In addition, there are some unusual items to consider, such as a welcoming door wreath (page 79), a violet-covered basket (page 91) and a candle-holding free-standing decoration made with roses, vegetables, fruit, and terracotta pots (page 95).

Whatever your choice, rest assured that such a bold decorative statement will be remembered long after the wedding is over.

Unusual decorations that make the most of bold colours will bring a welcome feeling of warmth to a winter or autumn wedding.

Door Wreath

A door wreath is an unusual item for decoration at a wedding, but greeting your guests at the entrance to the church or reception will make a wonderful impression. Set the scene for the entire wedding with this sumptuous display of warm, welcoming colours.

Before deciding to include such a wreath in your decorations, do make sure you have permission to attach it to the door of the church or the reception venue from the appropriate authorities. Often there are studs or nails already in place from which to hang it, or it may be possible to suspend it from a wire hanging from the top of the door, which means it is not necessary to make any mark on the door itself.

There are two types of wreath in the next few pages: the basic flower wreath explained in detail first, and a more elaborate double ring that is pictured on page 82.

The framework for the wreath is a wire frame that is covered with damp moss. As usual, it is necessary to tease out the moss first to remove any pieces of twig, large clods of earth or root balls. The moss is then firmly bound on to the frame with string or reel wire.

In addition to the foliage specified below, I have also used some lichen on my wreath. Lichen has always fascinated me, and its wonderful forms and colours are a joy to work with.

The pieces of lichen used here were collected in spring while staying on the west coast of Scotland. I could have filled the whole car easily as there was so much wonderful moss and lichen to see, but in the UK, picking these materials from anything other than private property is strictly forbidden.

<small>WHAT YOU WILL NEED</small>

1 x 45cm (18in) wire wreath frame • Moss • Twine or reel wire • Polythene • 18-gauge stub wire
Several stems trailing ivy • 12 stems leather-leaf fern • 10 stems hypericum berries • 6 stems red amaryllis
8 stems cerise pink amaryllis • 40 stems mixed anemones • 30 stems deep red roses
10 stems purple *Eustoma grandiflorum*

~ 1 ~

Cover the wreath frame with moss, using string or reel wire. Work round in an anti-clockwise direction until the whole frame is covered with a firmly attached layer. Cut strips of black polythene from a rubbish (trash) bag and pin these on to the back of the ring using short 'hairpins' of stub wire. This prevents the damp moss drying out, and more importantly, it stops damp or wires damaging the surface of the door.

Wire 10–13cm (4–5in) pieces of fern on a double-leg mount (see pages 18–19). Do the same with the hypericum foliage. Pin three of four strands of ivy on to the moss base, again using hairpins of wire, positioning it so as to cover as much of the moss as possible. Next add the ferns, hypericum and lichen, if you are using it.

~ 2 ~

Break the amaryllis heads from their stem and wire them up singly, on an 18-gauge wire using a double-leg mount (see pages 18–19). Push the wires into the moss until the ends protrude from the back of the base. Bend them back on to themselves so that the ends are covered by the moss base and will not scratch the door's surface.

Position the amaryllis flowers in clumps of three and five, grouping them by colour. Use the buds as well, but keep them within the edges of the design to prevent them sticking out and breaking up the clean edges of the finished circular arrangement.

~ 3 ~

Cut the mixed anemones very short and wire them up into small bunches of about four or five heads. Use them to cover up as much moss as possible, but keep checking the whole shape of the design to ensure it remains quite circular.

When wiring in the anemones pull the wires well into the moss to ensure the stem ends are touching the damp moss and are therefore able to take up water and remain fresh.

~ 4 ~

Wire up the rose heads into clumps of three or five, again on a double-leg mount (see pages 18–19). Use these in groups to fill in any gaps remaining. One or two single heads may be useful to help cover the wires used to attach the amaryllis.

Once complete, spray thoroughly with fresh cold water and place in a box of damp tissue paper until required.

NEXT PAGE *As a variation it is often possible to use two rings which can either both be of flowers or, as here, one of flowers and one using fruits and vegetables. This obviously increased the display, and looks good on a large door.*
A ring of big fruit, such as apples and pears, can become very heavy, so choose your materials with care.
Here I have used radiccio, lollo rosso lettuce, red onions, apples, plums, cherry tomatoes, aubergines, red peppers, black grapes and strawberries. All were wired individually and attached to a mossed base in the way described above.

Candelabra

Some churches do not seem to be suitable for a formal style of pedestal arrangement: they can often appear too formal and contrived. One way around this, and to still create an imposing decoration is to decorate a candlestick or candelabra. These are particularly suitable if the wedding is in winter, or late in the day, when the golden, flickering light from a group of candles will give a wonderful warmth to the church.

WHAT YOU WILL NEED
Candelabra • Oasis • Chicken wire • Stub wires • Candles • 10 stems trailing ivy
20 stems silver dollar eucalyptus • 10 stems leather-leaf fern • 5 stems deep red amaryllis
5 stems cerise pink amaryllis • 10 stems Bells of Ireland (molucella) • 10 stems hypericum berries
30 stems purple *Eustoma grandiflorum* • 15 stems red gerbera • 40 stems 'Only Love' roses

~ 1 ~

A large wrought-iron candelabra holding about thirteen candles has had four chicken-wire-wrapped blocks of Oasis attached to its central pole. Wire stems of trailing ivy into a bunch and attach it underneath the Oasis so that it trails down the stem of the candelabra.

Add the candles to ensure they are secure, and so that none of the foliage or flowers will be in the flames.

Silver dollar eucalyptus with its rich red stems is used as the main foliage, with leather-leaf fern to help cover the Oasis.

~ 2 ~

Stems of rich, deep red and cerise pink amaryllis are added next. Because their stems are so thick it is advisable to put them in before the Oasis becomes too crowded. Use a piece of cane or your forefinger to first make a pilot hole into the Oasis in which you can then gently push the amaryllis stem.

A bunch of clear green molucella is next added, to help lift the foliage a little and prevent the whole from becoming too dark and heavy. I also added some red hypericum berries for a different shape and texture.

~ 3 ~

Some deep purple *E.grandiflorum* works
well with this strong colouring, and its
beautiful grey foliage contrasts with the
eucalyptus. Try to use it in groups so that
it will be noticeable, and allow it to
protrude slightly.

~ 4 ~

Bright red gerbera with golden centres
are added next, and finally, clumps of
deep red 'Only Love' roses complete this
sumptuous and lush arrangement.

Small posies of the same flowers have
been tied with raffia to the choir-stall
candlesticks, and once everything is lit
the whole church looks magical.

Buttonholes and Corsages

Flowers for a man's buttonhole (boutonniere) or a lady's corsage are the ultimate finishing touch for a perfect wedding celebration. Because they are small they need not be expensive, but the blooms and surrounding leaves used should be carefully selected so as to be utterly perfect. Many different combinations of flowers and foliage are possible: for further ideas see the photographs on page 90.

I often think that if I had a choice, life in the 1920s would have been great fun — but only for the wealthy. It seems such an elegant era, with every gentleman going to work with a fresh flower in his buttonhole, and with corsages of beautiful orchids, fragrant roses or heady gardenias being *de rigueur* for the lady on her way to an evening out at the opera or a dinner party.

Such constant demand must have helped to keep florists of the day busy, for then, as now, buttonholes (boutonnieres) and corsages are time-consuming to make and yet never very expensive to buy.

It is often a good idea to allocate the flowers for buttonholes and corsages at the time of conditioning your flowers so that you are able to select the most perfect of blooms. This is often no easy task and you may have to go through several stems before you find enough that are not crushed, torn or blemished. Allow your chosen stems a roomy bucket to prevent the flowers or leaves from any further damage.

To help clear up any confusion over etiquette, a gentleman wears a buttonhole on his left lapel, and a lady wears a corsage on her right and often with the stem uppermost, though this is of course, a matter of taste. Remember that seat belts often cut across your shoulder and jacket front just at the height of the buttonhole, so wait until you reach your destination before putting it on.

WHAT YOU WILL NEED

FOR ONE BUTTONHOLE • 1 rose, opening and undamaged • 3 perfect rose leaves • Silver wire
Stub wire • Gutta-percha tape • Pin

~ 1 ~

Having selected a rose which is in
perfect condition and just beginning to
open, carefully cut off its stem, leaving
about 3.5cm (1 1/2in).

Holding the flower carefully so as not to
bruise the petals, insert a stub wire up the
stem until you feel it enter the calyx.
Push the end of a silver wire into the side
of the calyx and bend it down the stem.
Secure the silver wire to the stub wire,
winding it around both the flower's stem
and the wire.

~ 2 ~

Select three perfect leaves. One of the
leaves should be slightly larger than the
other two.

Working with the largest leaf first, turn it
so that the back of the leaf is facing
towards you. Pierce the back of the leaf
with a silver wire, as if taking a tiny
stitch across the central vein. Then bend
the wires down to form a hairpin shape.
Bind one wire around the other, trapping
and securing the stem-end as you bind.
Do the same for all the leaves.

Bind over the wire 'stem' with gutta-
percha tape, to conserve moisture within
the leaf and hide the wires, giving the
finished piece a more natural effect.

~ 3 ~

Arrange the three leaves to suit the flowers, generally with the slightly larger one at the back. The wire at the back of the leaf will enable you to gently curve the leaves, thus framing the flower to give a pleasing effect.

Once you have the leaves in position, carefully bind them to the rose stem using gutta-percha tape.

~ 4 ~

Once taped, cut the combined 'stem' to within approximately 7.5cm (3in) of the rose head.

Carefully insert a pin into the calyx of the rose, gently spray it with clean cold water and put into a tissue-covered box until required.

NEXT PAGE It is possible to make a huge variety of corsages using all sorts of different flowers and colours. For example: plain white stephanotis (top left), simple violets (top right), and a perfect red rose with violets, hypericum and lichen (bottom left). Always make sure that your flowers are perfect, and put them together following the steps above. Corsages are best stored in nests of damp tissue paper until required (bottom right).

Floral Basket

This charming yet versatile basket can be scaled up or down, depending on the type of flower used for covering, and the size of the decoration required. It can look wonderful on a small scale for a young bridesmaid to carry. Although violets are the choice here, you could also use primroses, lily of the valley, stephanotis, paper-white narcissi or Christmas rose (Helleborus niger); and fill it with pot-pourri, fresh petals, decorative vegetables, or an additional flower arrangement.

WHAT YOU WILL NEED
1 basket, approximately 25cm (10in) diameter • Chicken wire (see page 16) • Moss • Stub wires
Reel wire • 60–80 bunches violets (or alternatively primroses, lily of the valley, stephanotis, paper-white
narcissi or Christmas rose)• Polished red apples

~ 1 ~

Cut a piece of chicken wire into a circular shape to cover the base and outsides of the basket, with an extra 5cm (2in) overlap over into the basket. Stand the basket on the chicken wire, and lay a band of teased, damp moss around the base. Pull up one side of the wire and bend the ends over into the middle of the basket, trapping the moss between the basket's exterior and the chicken wire. Ensure the moss is evenly distributed to prevent bumps and bulges appearing in the finished product.

Also bind moss firmly on to the handle of the basket, using either twine or reel wire. Be careful not to make the handle too thick. The moss here is only to give some moisture to the flowers and so it does not need to be too bulky.

~ 2 ~

Leaving them in bunches, cut the violets' stems very short and wire them on to a 20-gauge wire, with a double-leg mount (see pages 18–19). It is easier to wire all the bunches first, before beginning to cover the basket: that way you don't have to keep stopping to wire up more.

Once wired, work quickly to cover the sides of the basket by pushing the wires through the basket and bending them back into the moss base to ensure the bunches are securely fastened. Make sure the top rim of the basket is covered generously with flowers.

~ 3 ~

To decorate the basket handle, take the violets out of the bunches, leaving the stems as long as possible but removing any leaves. Working up and across the handle with groups of about 12–15 stems at a time, gently bind them on to the mossed handle using binding wire or string. Cover all sides of the handle as you work across it. Pull the wire tightly to secure the stems, but make sure you are not garotting the flower heads.

~ 4 ~

Ensure the basket is evenly covered, including the handle. Any small gaps can be filled with small bunches wired up and pushed into place. Place some moss in the bottom of the basket and fill it with polished red apples. Oranges and apples would also create a wonderful effect.

Violets are unusual in that they take up water through their flower heads, so generously spray the whole basket with water, cover with wet tissue and place in a sealed plastic bin liner (trash bag) until it is required.

Fruit and Vegetable Pot

Here is an ideal opportunity to make the most of the decorative qualities of fruit and vegetables, combined with the sumptuous colours of deep red roses and violets. The unusual forms and colours of all the materials are beautifully highlighted by a thick beeswax candle. This decorative arrangement could be used on its own on a buffet table or in a window niche of a church, or grouped on the chancel steps or at the entrance of your reception venue.

In the winter months, supplies of all sorts of fruit and vegetables are flown in from around the world ensuring a plentiful array of wonderfully exotic materials at a fraction of the cost of out-of-season flowers. The colours, textures and especially the shapes of many fruits and vegetables are wonderfully inspirational, and can be great fun to work with for very eye-catching decorations.

For this arrangement, two Victorian terracotta pots have been stacked inside each other to form a solid and stable base. Oasis and moss provide the support for materials, which are either wired, or held up on short bamboo skewers.

This is a great opportunity to be bold and inventive, and here I have used everything from stems of rosemary, to blackberries and aubergines (eggplants) to asparagus.

It is essential that this arrangement is worked all around – even if it is only going to be seen from one side (front facing) – to ensure that it remains stable and will not overbalance.

Whatever its eventual use, here is a decoration that is equally rewarding to create and to look at.

WHAT YOU WILL NEED

2 x 20cm (8in)-wide Victorian terracotta pots • Moss • Polythene • Oasis • Chicken wire
Bamboo skewers • 1 x 4cm (1⅝in)-diameter beeswax candle • 10 short stems rosemary
Fruit: satsumas (tangerines), apples, strawberries, raspberries, plums, physalis (chinese gooseberry),
cherry tomatoes, blackberries • Vegetables: miniature aubergines (eggplants), round and long radishes,
asparagus 10 stems red roses • 3 bunches violets

~ 1 ~

Stack the two pots, one inside the other,
and pack the gap with moss. Line the
upper pot with polythene and wedge a
piece of soaked Oasis into the top. Cover
it with chicken wire (see page 16). Place
the candle firmly in the centre of the
Oasis.

Short sprigs of rosemary are added in
clumps. Satsumas (tangerines) and apples
have been wired with a double-leg mount
(see pages 18–19) on an 18-gauge 30cm
(12in) stub wire. They are added in
clumps of three.

~ 2 ~

Plums, miniature aubergines (eggplants)
and radishes are wired and added, again
in groups. The fruits will have much
more impact if they are used in clumps
rather than dotted singly throughout
the design.

Stems of asparagus look wonderful
because they are so different in shape
from the other spherical fruits
used so far.

~ 3 ~

Physalis, cherry tomatoes and
strawberries are impaled on long bamboo
skewers and added, studding the
arrangement. Again, they are placed in
groups for maximum impact.

~ 4 ~

Fill in any gaps in the Oasis using short
stems of red roses and clusters of violets
wired together.

Spray the whole with a fine mist of clean
cool water, wrap in damp tissue paper,
and put to one side until required.

Wedding Four

THE GRAND AFFAIR

St Mary of The Fields, Cripplegate, London EC2

THE TRADEMARK OF A GRAND WEDDING seems to be the watchwords 'less is more'.

Often I am presented with a huge church and a very grand, almost austere, reception venue. Large spaces require substantial arrangements, so it is usually better to create a small number of focal points in a building than to try and fill the whole space with smaller arrangements which can so easily be lost or overlooked once it is crowded with people.

Arrangements on a large scale can be great fun, giving enormous scope to use all sorts of materials. Flowering rose plants and/or trees and shrubs can be packed into an urn along with bunches of tall lilies and roses to create sumptuous displays. Massive church candlesticks provide the ideal base upon which to build a thick collar of flowers.

However, with such large arrangements, you must be careful about which flowers you decide to include and therefore which colour scheme you will use. For example, be aware that blues and purples recede. If you fill a dark room with spires of dark blue delphinium, from the end of the room it might look as if there were no flowers at all.

In large arrangements it is also often best to use more of one type of flower. A vast sandstone urn full of one type of lily or rose can be much more of a statement than if you put in half a dozen different types of flower and foliage.

Look around you at the architecture and the fabric of the building. The rooms should provide you with some inspiration for planning your decorations. For example, there may be huge swags of foliage carved in the wood or stone. Are

Delicate 'Golden Shower' orchids, jasmine and nephro fern are an ideal combination for a lady's corsage. Instructions for making corsages can be found on pages 87-89.

there any areas where you could copy this in fresh plant material?

Many larger churches tend to have a high altar, and one further down the nave where the actual ceremony takes place. If this is the case, focus attention on this second altar by positioning your major arrangements to act as a frame to the bride and groom. Obviously, you must ensure that they do not obscure the view of the congregation, nor must they get in the way of the clergy.

Another excellent place to position a pair of arrangements, or one large one, is at the back of the church opposite the end of the aisle. It may not be seen when the congregation arrives at the church as people are anxious to be shown to their seats and will be busy seeing what hymns have been chosen and trying to spot people they know. However, as they walk back down the aisle at the end of the service it will be the first thing they see, and if the inevitable queue forms, people will usually have plenty of time to look at the flowers.

In the film, if you look very closely at the scenes preceding the wedding you will catch a glimpse of me in the only acting role I'm qualified for: that of a florist, carrying a box of flowers into the church. So I can quite honestly say that I actually appeared in *Four Weddings and a Funeral.*

Yellow 'Texas' roses combined with yellow lilies add a bright splash of colour to any venue.

Group Arrangement

A tall, free-standing arrangement of interesting foliage and glorious, bright flowers creates a noticeable impact that cannot be achieved with lots of small decorations. People will be standing for much of the time, so a large arrangement will still be seen over all the heads — and hats.

When undertaking a large, arrangement such as this, it is essential to use a stable, secure base in which you are fully confident. However, occasionally even the most experienced of us will have an arrangement that may become unbalanced. If so, a couple of large stones or house bricks can be useful to add to the back of the design to keep it upright.

The container used here is an urn and plinth that is made from reconstituted sandstone. It is exceedingly heavy which means that though awkward to transport, it provides a good solid base for this type of arrangement.

Do not feel that it is essential to cram the entire arrangement full of flowers. With a display like this it is as pleasing to the eye to notice the foliage as to cover it over with masses of flowers. One of the first things I ever remember being told by George Smith, the world-famous NAFAS judge and demonstrator who has become a great friend and mentor over the years, was 'to leave room for the butterflies'.

By allowing space you are able to enjoy the colour and the form of the flowers, which is very satisfying when they are as lovely a mixture as is used here.

WHAT YOU WILL NEED
Urn or other container • Bowl to hold Oasis • Oasis blocks • 5cm (2in)-mesh chicken wire
Galvanized wire (for attaching rose plants) • Moss • Extension tubes (see page 17)
8 stems rhododendron foliage • 15 young silver birch branches • 8 stems white leaf (sorbus) • 5 stems dill
2 climbing rose plants: 'Dreaming Spires' and 'Laura' • 10 stems guelder rose (*Viburnum opulus*)
5 stems angelica • 50 stems 'Texas' roses • 20 stems white phlox • 25 sunflowers
15 stems flowering oil-seed rape (*Brassica napus*)• 10 stems 'Casa Blanca' lilies • 20 stems longiflorum lilies
10 stems trailing ivy

~ 1 ~

Fill the bowl with soaked Oasis, secure it with chicken wire and wedge it firmly into the urn with damp moss.

Begin by placing your foliage, in lengths that will establish the size and outline of the finished arrangement.

Work from the very back of the Oasis to the front. Do not work from the middle of the bowl as this will result in a very front-heavy design that may topple over.

Add the foliage: contrasting rhododendron and branches of young silver birch.

~ 2 ~

The joy of creating such a large arrangement means that one can add whole plants. Here, the root balls of two climbing rose plants have been wrapped in black polythene. They are wired into the arrangement with galvanized wire.

Do not worry about hiding the black polythene at this stage. It will become camouflaged, and if it is still visible later, a handful of moss or bunch of ivy trails will easily cover it.

Fresh-looking guelder rose and angelica stems are added into the centre.

~ 3 ~

Make up bunches of roses and phlox and place them in the extension tubes. Ensure that each tube of flowers is well positioned with its spike firmly and securely embedded into the main blocks of Oasis. Also, make sure that the flowers all appear to spring from the same central point, in order to create a pleasing and well-balanced arrangement.

~ 4 ~

Add the principal flowers, in this case sunflowers. They are grouped to create the most impact. Do not forget to cut some shorter and recess them to the centre to create depth. Also add some bright yellow lilies and three extension tubes of flowering oil-seed rape. The final flowers are enormous stems of fragrant 'Casa Blanca' and longiform lilies, placed in groups. Use these last as they damage very easily indeed.

Add a bunch of ivy to cover the polythene, if necessary, and to lead the eye down the design.

Tied-bunch Pew ends

Bunches of perfect roses give a novel shape to church pew decorations. They are presented very simply in a generous bunch with a mass of flowers separated by just a little foliage. Although the rose stems are tied tightly with twine, when finished they appear to be held in place by a rope of fresh green moss. The moss both hides the binding twine, and supports the rose heads, giving an uncomplicated yet stylish finish.

Some churches have removed their traditional wooden pews and replaced them with chairs. Although this allows the building to be much more multi-functional, it does tend to cause some problems for the florist. The original pews were still in place for this wedding ceremony – the disastrous dénouement for Charles (Hugh Grant) and his intended bride, nicknamed 'Duck Face' – but we decided to have a different and unusual look for the pew decorations.

Again, these can be made in advance, but once arranged, they should be stood in buckets of water until it is time to decorate the church, as there is no water-retaining material in the arrangement that allows the flowers to get moisture once they are hung up. It is advisable to position them only on the morning of the wedding as once they are in place they will gradually begin to wilt and dry out .

Remember that the bunch is to be 'flat-backed': it does not need flowers on all sides as the back will be against the side of the pew or the chair.

The bunch is attached to the pew using a double length of reel wire. Take the middle of the wire around the back of the pew end. Hold the bunch in the desired position, pass the two ends of the wire over the bunch, just beneath the moss rope, and twist them together tightly. Cut off the ends, and push them back on themselves into the moss rope to prevent anyone catching their clothes on them.

WHAT YOU WILL NEED

FOR EACH PEW END • 20 'Texas' stem roses • 3–5 stems ming or asparagus fern foliage
Moss • Reel wire • Twine

~ 1 ~

Begin by preparing the roses. Remove all the thorns and most of the foliage, but leave the topmost leaves to help add body to the design.

You may choose to wear gloves for de-thorning as it can be a painful task. I tend to work down the stems picking off each thorn by hand. This is a fiddly process, but you will become quicker with practice. There are other ways to remove thorns but as they involve scraping the stem, causing unsightly marking, I would advise against them.

~ 2 ~

Take a piece of taller foliage and four or five roses, and arrange them in an arc shape. Decide now on the finished size of the arc, as these first placements are at the outer edge of the design. Tie a length of twine around these stems and make sure it holds them securely in place.

Gradually add more of the roses, a stem at a time. Use the foliage to help lift the flower heads and keep them separate.

As you position each new stem of foliage or rose, give a single turn around the stems with the twine and pull it taut to prevent the flowers slipping. Gradually build up your bunch into a pleasing and regular shape and tie off the twine.

~ 3 ~

Put the bunch to one side and make up
the moss binding.

Begin by forming a sausage of fresh
carpet moss. Wrap the end of the reel
wire around it and gently but firmly bind
the roll to create a rope of moss about
25–30cm (10–12in) in length. Finish off
the wire at the end, leaving about
30cm (12in) for fixings.

~ 4 ~

Attach the moss rope around the bunch,
covering the binding string. Wire the
ends of the rope together at the back,
making sure you do not leave any ends of
wire protruding to scratch the pew end
or chair.

Attach the bunch to the pew (see page
107), being careful not to mark the wood
or leave any protruding ends of wire.

Pillar Arrangement

Here is an excellent way of providing a clearly visible yet discreet decoration that is also economical on space. It allows your beautiful and valuable flowers to be displayed to perfection giving everyone an uninterrupted view that is often hard to achieve with a large group of people. Also called 'flower drops' these arrangements often work well as a pair, although one on its own can look equally attractive.

Some churches or reception venues have no particular areas where a group or pedestal arrangement would be suitable. Other churches are too narrow in the aisles to allow room for any floor-standing decoration. If this is the case, often a pillar decoration or 'flower drop' is the ideal solution.

Pillar decorations can be hung high so that they are easy to see over a large group of people, and they are in no danger of being knocked over by the bridal party or over-enthusiastic guests.

Most buildings will have some wall space or architectural features which are suitable for hanging such an arrangement, but it is absolutely imperative to find adequate fixing without having to knock nails into valuable wood or easily marked features of the building.

It is as well to be aware that this sort of construction contains no Oasis or water-retaining material other than damp moss. It should, therefore, be made towards the end of your work time to ensure the flowers are as fresh as possible on the day.

As this arrangement contains lilies you should be aware of the danger of pollen marking people's clothing. However, if the arrangement is to be hung somewhere where it will not be brushed against as people walk past, it is preferable to leave the pollen-covered stamens in the lily flowers as they add so much to the character of the bloom.

WHAT YOU WILL NEED

Chicken wire • Moss • Stub wires • 10 stems trailing ivy • 20 stems cream lily • 30 stems 'Texas' rose
10 stems solidaster • 5 stems leather-leaf fern • 10 stems 'Golden Shower' orchid

~ 1 ~

Make up a chicken-wire base approx
90cm (3ft) long and about 18cm (7in)
wide. It should look like a flattened
sausage, with a flat back (see
pages 20–21).

Begin by pinning on to it the ivy trails
using hairpins of stub wire. Try to cover
as much of the base as possible with the
ivy and add the leather-leaf fern to assist
in camouflaging your base.

~ 2 ~

Wire up stems of solidaster in double-leg
mounts (see pages 18–19). Do them all
before you begin to arrange them. Then
position them throughout the
decoration. As you work ensure you
maintain a regular shape to the design.

Next wire up the 'Golden Shower'
orchids as above, and put them into
position. Do not forget to push the wires
back into the moss base to ensure they
do not scratch anything.

~ 3 ~

Using a couple of stems of lily at a time, both buds and open flowers, mount them on to a double-leg mount and wire them into the base, ensuring they are securely anchored. Be careful not to crush the petals as they will mark very easily.

If necessary, remove the pollen from the lily stamens (see page 111).

~ 4 ~

Wire the 'Texas' roses into clumps of three and five, and add them to the finished arrangement, recessing some of them into the other flowers and foliage, in order to create depth.

Once completed, spray the entire arrangement with water and cover it with damp tissue paper until required.

Bride's Bouquet

A classically beautiful bouquet in white and green is made from fragrant roses, lily of the valley, jasmine, stephanotis and perfect lilies. It is a great honour to be asked to make a bride's bouquet, and the result will live on for years to come in treasured photographs of the day.

Making the bridal flowers is one of my favourite tasks. However it is a huge responsibility, and an inexperienced florist should think long and hard before undertaking this task. A bouquet must be made at the very last minute so if there are any dramas or problems, there is very little time to rectify a difficult situation.

It is vital to establish the style, size and design of the flowers well in advance of the wedding day. Attending a dress fitting is a good idea, and samples of the fabric are extremely useful for colour matching. It is also a great help if the bride can show you a magazine photograph or draw a sketch of the design she would like.

Co-ordinate all the flowers and foliage well in advance, and ensure the flowers are all perfect. I tend to order twice as many lilies and roses as I need to ensure I will have sufficient perfect, open blooms on the day. Lilies need to be purchased well in advance to give the flowers time to open, and it is necessary to remove the stamens to prevent pollen marking either petals or dress.

Judging when to buy flowers only comes with experience. One general rule is that once a flower has opened, it can always be put into a dark, cool room for a while to prevent it from blooming, but tight rose or lily buds are hard to open, so buy well ahead: early is better than late.

WHAT YOU WILL NEED

Stub wires • Silver reel wire • Stem-binding tape • 10 lengths trailing ivy (in immaculate condition)
5 short pieces variegated pittosporum • 8–10 stems ivy-leafed geraniums • 100 heads stephanotis
15 stems white spray rose • 30 stems 'Teneka' roses • 3 jasmine plants • 100 stems lily of the valley
7–10 heads and some buds 'Casa Blanca' lily • 2 stephanotis plants, unravelled from their wire hoop,
cut and conditioned for 24 hours

~ 1 ~

Wire up all the flowers and foliage: the stephanotis in bunches of 12–14 flowers, the jasmine in clumps and the lily of the valley in bunches of 12–15 stems. Bind the wires with stem-binding tape right to the end.

Put together the framework, to define the size and shape of the bouquet. Use the stephanotis trails as your main frame, concentrating the flowers at the centre and also using some to take your eye to the tip of the bouquet. Add the ivy-leafed geranium, and bind all the wired stems together using silver reel wire.

~ 2 ~

Add the smaller, looser flowers: the spray roses and jasmine. These create a definite shape for your bouquet but are not the focal flowers. The spray roses are used at the edge, with one or two stems towards the centre. This leaves the centre clear to use the focal flowers and prevents the bouquet becoming crowded.

Do not worry if some of the roses are in bud and others are in bloom. I always leave the heads on if the petals have dropped off, as the stamen-covered seed heads are still very attractive.

~ 3 ~

The wired bunches of stephanotis are
added next. Use them at the top towards
the back of the bouquet and allow them
to protrude slightly. Then add some
white rose flowers, recessing them
slightly to create depth. Next use the
wired-up clumps of flowering jasmine.

Remember to keep trimming the ends of
the wire as you go to prevent a huge
bundle of wires forming, which will not
only be heavy but also be hard to cut
through in one go.

~ 4 ~

Put the wired bunches of lily of the
valley at the top of the bouquet. I always
tend to concentrate the lily of the valley
at the top in this way, preferring to keep
it upright, as it grows. Being such a tiny,
delicate flower it needs to be used in
clumps or it will become lost.

~5~

The last flowers to be added are the 'Casa Blanca' lilies. These are such fragile blooms that they need to be handled with great care, and by putting them in last you can avoid as much damage as possible. Use some buds, too, for they have wonderful shapes and colours. The weight of the flower heads may mean you have to wire them on to several lengths of stub wire to ensure they remain upright.

~6~

Finish the bouquet by filling in any holes with small foliage pieces wired into clumps. Pull them deep into the bouquet so as no to cover the flowers.

Last, cover the handle (made of amalgamated wires) with stem-binding tape and finally with ribbon or, if available, a piece of fabric from the dress. Finish with a small, discreetly wired bow attached to the top of the handle at the back of the bouquet.

Lightly spray the bouquet with a very fine mist. Be sure to store it safely out of the reach of pets or small people.

Top Table Arrangement

This opulent yet restrained collection of green, white and cream has been made into a decorative border that is ideal for a long top table at a wedding breakfast. Its subtle colours will both ornament and frame the all-important bridal party.

The top table is always a focus of attention during a formal wedding breakfast. However, as the speeches will probably be made from behind it, the flowers should act as a frame for the speakers without obscuring anyone's view. This low arrangement is easy to construct by using a number of flower-supporting trays that are lined up to look like a long, single display.

When arranging your reception it is essential to ensure that the cloth – of whatever colour you chose – is properly ironed prior to use to remove any strong creases. It should be hung neatly over the front and the sides of the table, with the edges all at the same length, just touching the floor.

This arrangement has among its flowers some anthurium which some people dislike, feeling that it looks artifical. When filming the second wedding in *Four Weddings*, Maggie Grey, the production designer, asked for a plant to dress the corner of a room. I sent up a huge anthurium plant. Because it had no flowers on it, I had added some cut ones in planted tubes of water. Maggie came down saying it worked fine after she had removed all the plastic flowers. It took some convincing before she believed they were real, and that they grow from a plant exactly like the one I'd sent her.

For an average top table seating twelve people, you will need at least six trays as specified below.

WHAT YOU WILL NEED

FOR ONE TRAY • 1 x 35cm (14in)-long Oasis tray • 1 1/2 blocks Oasis (see page 16) • 5 stems box foliage
5 stems sprengerii fern • 3 stems ligularia leaves • 5 stems antirrhinum (snapdragon) • 3 stems anthurium
5 stems white campanula • 10 stems cream Singapore orchids • 5 stems cream gerbera
1 stem 'Casa Blanca' lily • 20 stems 'Teneka' white roses • 5 stems tuberose • 5 stems cow parsley

~ 1 ~

Strap blocks of soaked Oasis on to the trays and line them up on your work bench as they will be, once in place. Try to work on them in this position, or if you do not have space, work on them a pair at a time. This will mean that your finished decoration looks as if it is all one thing, with no gaps between the trays.

Box foliage has a wonderful strong dark green colour, and is useful for covering Oasis without becoming too dense. Added to it is sprengerii fern, which is very light and trails beautifully. Use this in the front and less in the middle of your arrangement, so that it will fall over the table front to soften the edge.

A few beautiful glossy dark ligularia leaves have been added to create focus and act as a foil to the delicate flowers.

~ 2 ~

Add the antirrhinum, white campanula and Singapore orchids. Use them at the front of the Oasis to hang over the table edge, but also use some throughout the rest of the decoration. You must arrange the whole of the tray, not just the front, to ensure even distribution of weight. Otherwise the tray may become front-heavy and fall forward. You must also remember that those people sitting at the top table should not just see a mass of foliage and Oasis.

~ 3 ~

Beautiful cream gerbera and perfect
white 'Casa Blanca' lilies are added, fairly
randomly throughout, to create focal
points in the design. Keep them quite
short and remember not to make the
arrangement too tall in the centre or
people's views will be obscured.

~ 4 ~

White roses, fragrant tuberose, with its
delicate pink-tipped buds, and white cow
parsley are added to complete the
design, filling in any large or obvious
gaps. A few stems of green anthurium
give some relief from all the cream and
white, and provide a link with the green
of the foliage.

Once you have completeed your trays,
label them in order with little wired flags
of paper numbered 1–6. This means that
once you arrive at the reception they can
be placed on the top table in the order
they were arranged so that your
decoration will look like one long
garland of flowers.

List of Suppliers

UNITED KINGDOM

CUT FLOWERS

John Austin and Co Ltd.
305 Flower Market
New Covent Garden
London SW8 5NB
Tel 0171 720 6835

Baker and Duguid
(Covent Garden) Ltd.
286–7 Flower Market
New Covent Garden
London SW8 5NB
Tel 0171 720 6831

C M Grover Ltd.
304 Flower Market
New Covent Garden
London SW8 5NB
Tel 0171 498 0070

M & P Flowers Ltd.
N4 Flower Market
New Covent Garden
London SW8 5NB
Tel 0171 498 3034

Romede Flowers Ltd.
F2 Flower Market
New Covent Garden
London SW8 5NB
Tel 0171 720 0199

FOLIAGE & MOSSES

A & F Bacon
328 Flower Market
New Covent Garden
London SW8 5NB
Tel 0171 720 1843

PLANTS

Arnott and Mason
(Horticulture) Ltd.
255/257 Flower Market
New Covent Garden
London SW8 5NB
Tel 0171 720 7651

OTHER MATERIALS

Anita Taylor
Antique flowerpots,
baskets and containers
Yacht Harbour Cottage
7 Thorney Road
Emsworth, Hants
PO10 8BL
Tel 01243 378590

Patio
Terracotta pots from
France and Italy; plants,
shrubs and dried flowers
155 Battersea Park Road
London SW8 4BU
Tel 0171 622 8262

EQUIPMENT

Cocquerels Sundries Ltd
313–14 Flower Market
New Covent Garden
London SW8 5NF
Tel 0171 720 9121/2

UNITED STATES

FLORISTS

Aster Florists
1700 17th St.
Washington, D.C.
(202)-387-0092

Atlanta Floral Arts
318 Sandy Spring St.
Atlanta, GA 30328
(404)-252-2611

J. Barry Ferguson
Flowers
P.O Box 176
Oyster Bay, NY 11771
(516)-992-0005
mostly weddings

Bloomers
2975 Washington St.
San Francisco
CA 94115
(415)-563-3266

Bloomsbury Floral
Design
Los Angeles, CA
(213)-855-1001

Design by Jody
152 Baker Road
Lake Bluff, IL 60044
(708)-816-6661

Dulken and Derrick
12 West 21st St.
New York, NY 10010
(212)-929-3614
*specializes in floral designs to
match wedding attire; flowers
shipped nationwide*

The Empty Vase
2439 Westheimer St.
Houston, TX 77098
(713)-529-9969

Flowers & Co.
245 North Highway
Southampton
NY 11968
(516)-283-0777

The Flower Shop
616 North Almont
Drive
Los Angeles, CA 90069
(310)-274-8491

Gardenstyle
99 Via Mizner-Peruvian
Avenue
Palm Beach, FL 33480
(407)-655-2122
*specializes in party planning,
design, production, bouquets
and floral designs shipped
nationwide*

Glorimundi
107 West 28th St.
New York, NY 10001
(212)-695-4739

Green Valley Growers
10450 Cherry Ridge
Road
Sebastopol, CA 94572
(707)-823-5583
*floral designs and bridal
bouquets, flowers shipped
nationwide*

Greenworks
2015 Florida Avenue
Washington, D.C.
(202)-667-7570

Lisa Kreiger Gardens &
Interiors
P.O Box 221
Green Farms, CT 06436
(203)-259-8571
by appointment

Mark Turner
Flowers Ltd.
666 Pennsylvania Ave
Washington, D.C.
(202)-547-2020

Oppizzi
818 Greenwich Avenue
New York, NY 10011
(212)-633-2248

Paperwhite
415 West 23rd St.
New York, NY 10001
(212)-675-3599

Pure Mädderlake
478 Broadway
New York, NY 10013
(212)-941-7770
800-304-MADD

Robert Isabell, Inc.
410 West 13th St.
New York, NY 10011
(212)-645-7767

Jason Richards
363 W. Chicago Avenue
Chicago, IL 60610
(312)-664-0605

Rosedale Nurseries
51 Saw Mill Road
Hawthorne, NY 10532
(914)-769-1300

Dorothy Wako
15 West 26th St.
New York, NY 10010
(212)-685-5569
by appointment

Zezé Flowers
398 East 52nd St.
New York, NY 10022
(212)-753-7767/7768

MAIL ORDER

Garden Valley
Wholesale
(707)-792-0337
fax: (707)-792-0349
*garden roses May through
November; minimum order 60
stems*

SUPPLIES AND
FLORAL TOOLS

*(For foam, wire ribbon, tissue,
moss, spray paint, shears,
planters etc)*

Chelsea Market Ltd.
141 West 28th St.
New York, NY 10001
(212)-594-8286

Union County Florist
Supplies Inc.
800-221-6144

Index

Acknowledgements

Thank you is so easy to say, but when it touches your emotions it means so much more, and composing this list of thanks has been a telling experience for so many friends have been so kind and generous, not only with their houses and buildings for which they care, but with their time and talent.

I would never have become the florist I am now were it not for the teaching, encouragement and nurturing of several people, three in particular. First, Norma Richards, from my home town of Warwick and a close friend, who first taught me the rudiments of floristry, and who I still enjoy working with. Mr George Smith, the world-renowned NAFAS demonstrator and judge, took the trouble to answer the first letter I wrote to him many years ago when I was 16 years old. He gave me a large amount of his time; allowing me to assist him in several of his incredible creations. The Easter Garden at York Minster was my first taste of large scale decorating. Through him I met the late and greatly missed Robert Day, possibly the most talented person I have ever known. Through Robert I learned a great deal about the art of floral decoration. His generosity of skills was only matched by his flair and extraordinary vision. Since his untimely death in 1993 the world has been a poorer place, and those of us who knew and loved him and his work still miss him.

Decorating with flowers is a tough job. It requires early starts and long busy days. One of a floral decorator's pet hates is the statement 'Oh, flower arranging, how lovely. What a lovely job you have!' True, we work with beautiful materials and we see some amazing places as a result of our work, but is is a hard physical job requiring great dedication. It is that dedication which I would like to acknowledge here:

Janie Heynes, for always being there whenever I needed her, for giving so much of her time and talent; for letting me take over her home on more than one occasion, filling her kitchen with lilies, and her sink with washing up. Somehow, having spent all day working with me, she still manages to produce a delicious supper and all with apparent ease. Thanks too to her husband David, and to Laura, Jules and Wilbur for always making me so welcome.

Ruth Harris, for being such a wonderful friend, and for all her hard work assisting me with the arrangements for this book.

Sandra Lane, for becoming such a good friend and for her exquisite photography. Flowers are such inately beautiful things that often only a little work was required by me for Sandra to capture their faerie aspect so well. Working with her has been a joy.

I must also acknowledge the following for their help in many ways. Father Anthony Hogg for being so generous in allowing us to film in his beautiful church, St James the Great in Haney, Oxfordshire. The Reverend Mark Everett and the authorities of Merton College Chapel, Oxford. The Reverend Cornish for allowing us the use of St James Church, Selham, West Sussex. Rosalind Fairman for the use of her beautiful home. Jane Moren, for her delicious lunch and for finding our country church. David Gorton of A & F Bacon (Foliage Suppliers); David, Charlie and Melvin of Romede Flowers; Chris, Dennis and Lee at John Austin Ltd; Roy Steptoe, my wonderful porter and the best packer of a car I have ever seen.

Thanks too to Mary Douglas, David Jones, Noel Minett, Jenny Lamberton and Mark Walker. Also thank you to Michele Beroni for lending her shirt to be photographed in.

Thanks must also go to Cindy Richards of Ebury Press for asking me to write this book. Her patience and the fun she has given to the whole project have made it a joy to work on. Also to Margot Richardson for organizing my hectic schedule and for turning my hasty scribble into readable text.

Last, and most decidedly not least, to Nicholas Cannon for being the still small voice of calm in my life, wonderfully remote from the world of flowers; able to listen to my ramblings and gently restore my sanity and strength.